MEET THE KEY WORKERS

WORKERS IN EMERGENCY SERVICES

BY
SHALINI VALLEPUR

KidHaven PUBLISHING

Published in 2024 by
KidHaven Publishing, an Imprint of Greenhaven Publishing, LLC
2544 Clinton St., Buffalo, NY 14224

Written by: Shalini Vallepur
Edited by: John Wood
Designed by: Jasmine Pointer

Cataloging-in-Publication Data

Names: Vallepur, Shalini.
Title: Workers in emergency services / Shalini Vallepur.
Description: New York : KidHaven Publishing, 2024. | Series: Meet the key workers | Includes glossary and index.
Identifiers: ISBN 9781534544451 (pbk) | ISBN 9781534544468 (library bound) | ISBN 9781534544475 (ebook)
Subjects: LCSH: Emergency medical services-- Juvenile literature | First responders-- Juvenile literature
Classification: LCC HV551.2 V35 2024 | DDC 362.18 --dc23

Manufactured in the United States of America

CPSIA compliance information: Batch #CSKH24: For further information contact Greenhaven Publishing LLC at 1-844-317-7404.

Please visit our website, www.greenhavenpublishing.com. For a free color catalog of all our high-quality books, call toll free 1-844-317-7404 or fax 1-844-317-7405.

Find us on

Image Credits

All images are courtesy of Shutterstock.com, unless otherwise specified. With thanks to Getty Images, Thinkstock Photo and iStockphoto.

Cover – VAKS-Stock Agency, Rawpixel.com, Drop of Light, solarus, Rvector, Anatolir, elenabsl, Jane Kelly, John Roman Images. 2–3 – Rawpixel.com. 4–5 – Craveleo, Pixel-Shot. 6–7 – OgnjenO, Lucky Business. 8–9 – M.Moira, Kaganovich Lena, Dee Angelo, VectorShow. 10–11 – Stuart Monk, meunierd, Piyawat Nandeenopparit, StreetVJ, Mountain Brothers, Photo Spirit, Black Creator 24. 12–13 – Monkey Business Images, Akimov Igor, Jaromir Chalabala, White Wolf, elenabsl, 14–15 – michaeljung, Monkey Business Images, curiosity, Ilya Bolotov. 16–17 – danielcgold, Monkey Business Images, Toa55, intararit, Viktoriyani. 18–19 – curiosity, Paul Brewer, Danny Bakker, SB_photos, Zentangle, 1494. 20–21 – Noska Photo, IV. andromeda, Mr. Luck, Mountain Brothers. 22–23 – wavebreakmedia, michaeljung, ChameleonsEye, Yindee.

CONTENTS

Words that look like **this** can be found in the glossary on page 24.

HERE TO HELP

There are lots of jobs in the world and each one is different. Some jobs are always needed. The people who do these jobs are called key workers.

Key can sometimes mean needed and important.

Postal workers are always needed to make sure we get mail.

Without key workers, we would not have the things we need to live safely, such as food and **services**.

PEOPLE IN

EMERGENCY SERVICES

An emergency is when something dangerous happens. This might be a fire or someone getting hurt. When there is a serious emergency, we call an emergency service for help.

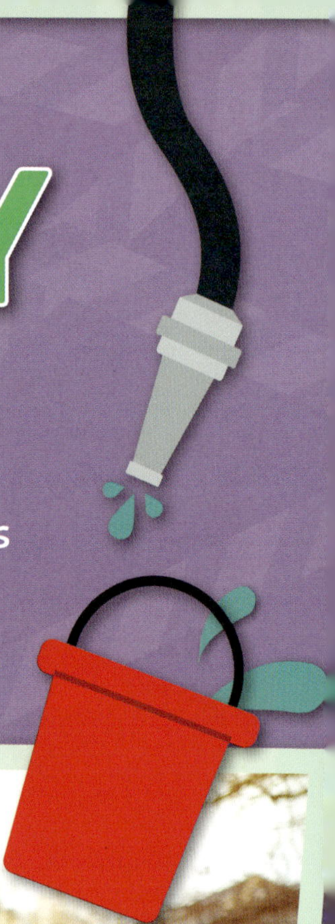

The people that work in emergency services are **trained** to help us. Let's learn all about the different people and jobs in emergency services!

ON THE

PHONE

When there is an emergency, we usually call for an emergency service using a phone. The person who answers the call will ask us what the emergency is, where it is, and if anyone is hurt.

They help us to stay calm.

Do you know how to call for an emergency service on the phone? Ask an adult to show you how to use a phone and what to say to an emergency **operator**.

Staying calm and knowing what to do in an emergency is important.

POLICE

Police **protect** us in all sorts of emergencies. If there is an **accident** or car crash on a road, traffic police can be called to help.

Police cars have loud **sirens** and flashing lights.

Some police officers protect us when there is a crime. They might be called to stop someone from stealing or causing trouble.

EMERGENCY HEALTH CARE

When somebody is badly hurt, we call for emergency health care. Ambulance drivers drive an ambulance to the hurt person and bring them to the hospital. They are trained to drive quickly but safely.

Ambulances have all the **equipment** and **medicine** needed in an emergency.

A pilot is trained to fly an air ambulance. Air ambulance helicopters can get to emergencies quickly and avoid the traffic on roads.

Paramedics are trained to give emergency treatment to people who are hurt. They may use the equipment in the ambulance to care for the hurt person and put them in the ambulance safely.

An emergency doctor helps people who are hurt or people who have been brought in by ambulance. Emergency nurses also help and explain what is happening to the hurt person.

FIREFIGHTERS

When there is a fire, we call for firefighters. Firefighters use fire engines to get to the emergency quickly. Fire engines have ladders on them and hoses for spraying water at fires.

Fire engine drivers have a very important job.

Fires are extremely dangerous. Firefighters are specially trained to put out fires. They wear special clothes that protect them from the heat.

Firefighters may also help in other emergencies, such as when people are trapped in cars or buildings.

COAST GUARD

The coast guard helps when there is an emergency at sea. Watch officers work in centers around the coast. They watch for any **distress signals**.

The coast guard drives rescue boats and helicopters. They are trained to rescue people who are stuck at sea. They also help keep other ships safe.

SEARCH AND RESCUE

Search and rescue is a service that looks for people who may be lost or in danger. They may look for people who need help after a **natural disaster** such as an earthquake or a flood.

Search dogs help to find people who are lost.

Search and rescue workers are often people who work for other services. Firefighters, police officers, and emergency health care workers may help search and rescue.

SAVING LIVES

Lots of different people work in emergency services to help keep us safe. Emergency services are there for us every single day.

Make sure you know how to call for emergency services. Ask an adult!

Now you know about some of the people who work in emergency services! Can you match each job below to the right person?

Fire engine driver

Drives fire engines

Traffic police

Helps with emergencies on the roads

Coast guard

Rescues people who are stuck at sea

GLOSSARY

accident	something that is not expected to happen which often ends in someone getting hurt or something being damaged
distress signals	messages or signs used to tell people you need help; they could be messages over radio
equipment	tools or machines that are used to do a certain job
medicine	something used or taken to fight off diseases
natural disaster	an event in nature that causes a lot of damage or harm, such as an earthquake
operator	someone who takes phone calls from people who need help and passes the information on to the right people
protect	to stop someone or something from being hurt or damaged
services	tasks or actions that people pay other people to do, such as caring for older people, fixing things that are broken, or cleaning
sirens	loud, repeating sounds to warn people of something, often used together with flashing lights
trained	having been taught how to do a job

INDEX